Faculty of Science and Engineering

Electrical and Electronic Engineering Department

Creation of Mail Server Based on Virtual Users and Domains with Postfix, Courier, Dovecot, MySQL

Supervised by:

Dr. Hidaia Alassouli

Student Name

Khumalo, Khumbulani V.

# Abstract

It is common these days for a single system to host many domains, for example uniswa.com and mtn.com or acme .com may run on a single host machine, but behave as if they were on three different hosts. A system usually has a canonical domain, it has its usual or local domain name, and additional domains are configured as virtual domains.

The purpose behind this work is to create a mail server solution based on Postfix that is based on virtual users and domains, i..e. users and domains that are in a MySQL database. The goal is to have completely virtual users and domains. bob@uniswa.com != bob@acme.com. This means creating a separate name spaces for reach domain.

It will also demonstrate the installation and configuration of Courier-Imap (IMAP/POP3), so it can authenticate against the same MySQL database Postfix uses. The resulting postfix server is capable of quota which is not built into Postfix by default; the project will demonstrate how to patch postfix appropriately. Passwords are stored in encrypted form in the database. The work also covers the installation of Mail Scanner, SpamAssassin and ClamAv so that emails will be scanned for spams and viruses. The administration of MySQL database can be done through a web based tool Postfixadmin or can be done manually in the MySQL shell. Postfixadmin is a web based management tool created for Postfix that handles Postfix style virtual domains and users that are stored in MySQL. The squirrelmail web based email client is installed, in order to check emails from anywhere in world via internet. All installations were done in Fedora 5 Linux machine.

# Table of contents

# 1. Introduction:

The purpose behind this project is to create a mail server solution based on Postfix that is based on virtual users and domains, i..e. users and domains that are in a MySQL database. It will also demonstrate the installation and configuration of Courier-Imap (IMAP/POP3), so it can authenticate against the same MySQL database Postfix uses. The resulting postfix server is capable of quota which is not built into Postfix by default; the project will demonstrate how to patch postfix appropriately. Passwords are stored in encrypted form in the database. The project also covers the installation of Mail Scanner, SpamAssassin and ClamAV so that emails will be scanned for spams and viruses. The administration of MySQL database can be done through a web based tool Postfixadmin or can be done manually in the MySQL shell. Postfixadmin is a web based management tool created for Postfix that handles Postfix style virtual domains and users that are stored in MySQL. The squirrelmail web based email client is installed, in order to check emails from anywhere in world via internet. All installations were done in Fedora 5 machine.

The project composed from the following parts:
• Installing Postfix.
• Installing Courier-IMAP (in case you want to use Courier as IMAP/POP Server).
• Creating the Database Tables.
• Populating Database with Some Data.
• Creating the Postfix-Mysql Configuration Files.
• Installing Postfixadmin.
• Installing MailScanner.
• Installing ClamAV and SpamAssassin.
• Creating the Virtual User and Virtual Directory.
• Configuring MailScanner.
• Configuring Postfix.
• Courier-IMAP Configuration.
• Configuring Squirrellmail.
• Testing the Configuration.

I advice that you install the necessary packages from rpm.pbone.net. All installations were done in Fedora 5 Linux machine.

## 2. Description of the Project:

### 2.1 Main Objectives:

The main objective of this work is to create an email server that supports mail delivery to multiple virtual domains .Each email address will be authentic to only that domain, for example Bob@mtn.com and Bob@acme.com are two different accounts that each receives different emails.

When the mail server setup has been completed it must be able to:

- Receive and store emails for users.
- Support quota to keep the mailboxes to a reasonable size of choice.
- Let users retrieve  emails through IMAP and POP3.
- Receive and forward email for users if they are authenticated.
- Offer a webmail interface to read emails in a web browser.
- Detect virus and spam emails and filter them out or tag them.

### 2.2 System Overview:

The project describes how to create an email server with virtual domains and virtual users (users who can not log into the system, they can only exist in a database).

Basic knowledge of the following components is required to successfully set up the server.

- MySQL (creating a database, granting access to users), this is a database system that stores information about the domains, the user accounts and email forwarding.
- SMTP (Postfix) this is a protocol used between mail servers to send email messages.
- POP3, IMAP the type used here is Courier-IMAP an alternative could be dovecot, this is a server that provides access to mail directories.
- Fedora (Linux), understanding the general system administration, using text editor, command line and reading log files.

The accounts are stored in a MySQL database .The domains will have separate name spaces, for example mail for Bob@acme.com and Bob@mtn.com will go to separate mailboxes. So the arrangement will be separate mailboxes for each virtual account.

The server will use a POP/IMAP server that supports multiple domains. In this arrangement the administrator need not create and maintain system accounts for email addresses on the server, instead he will configure Postfix to deliver mail to a local message store where each virtual email address can have its own mailbox file. The users then retrieve their messages through the POP /IMAP server.

In addition the server will be capable of quota support and scanning of spam and viruses (Mail Scanner, Spam Assassin). The database (MySQL) will be managed manually from the command line mysql shell or by a web based management tool (Postfixadmin) created for postfix, and the users access their emails through a web based email client interface client (Squirrelmail).The block diagram below (figure 1) illustrates the system.

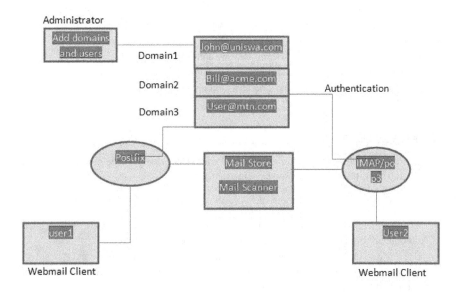

**Fig. 2.1 Server System Block Diagram**

## 2.3 Main Server Components:

The mail server will be created with the following packages in Fedora core 5 operating system:

- Postfix -2.2.8-1.2.

- MySQL -5.0.18-2.1.

- Courier – Imap – 4.4.1-1.5.

- Courier – Authlib – 0.62.1- 1.fc5.

- Squirrelmail – 1.4.6.tar.bz2.

- PostfixAdmin – 2.3.3.tar.gz.

- Apache2 that comes by default with Fedora core 5.

- Mail Scanner-4.84.3-1.rpm.tar.gz.

- Install-Clam-0.96.5-SA-3.3.1 or any clamav package.

- SpamAssassin which comes by default with Fedora core 5.

- Fedora core 5 (Operating system).

- Compaq 610 laptop   Intel core Duo 3GHz   2GB RAM 320 GB Hard Drive.

All packages used are the i386 types. It is assumed that Fedora core 5 and Mozilla Fire Fox have been successfully installed and support for HTTP and SMTP enabled with the Firewall turned off.

# 3. Main installation and configuration of the mail server packages:

The project covers the following parts:
• Installing Postfix.
• Installing Courier-IMAP (in case you want to use Courier as IMAP/POP Server).
• Creating the Database Tables.
• Populating Database with Some Data.
• Creating the Postfix-Mysql Configuration Files.
• Installing Postfixadmin.
• Installing MailScanner.
• Installing ClamAV and SpamAssassin.
• Creating the Virtual User and Virtual Directory.
• Configuring MailScanner.
• Configuring Postfix.
• Courier-IMAP Configuration.
• Configuring Squirrellmail.

## 3.1 Installing Postfix:

Postfix is not shipped with quota and MySQL databases support, so for it to support these a Postfix source package and a Postfix quota patch are obtained, extracted and the specification file of the patch edited as done below. Postfix is patched and a new Postfix package specific to the environment Postfix will run on is obtained. The new Postfix is then installed.

Download Postfix – 2.2.8 – 1.2.src.rpm and Postfix – 2.2.8 – vda.patch.gz or any other version in usr/redhat/SOURCES directory.

   #rpm -ivh Postfix – 2.2.8 – 1.2.src.rpm.

   #gunzip postfix-2.2.8-vda.patch.gz

   #cd /usr/src/redhat/SPECS/

   #gedit postfix.spec (editing the specification file)

   - change   % define MYSQL 0 to % define MYSQL 1

   - add   Patch 0: postfix-2.2.8-vda.patch to the # Patches stanza

   - add %patch0 -p1 -b .vda to the %setup -q stanza

Then build a new postfix package with quota and MySQL databases support and install it.

   #rpmbuild -ba postfix.spec

8

Navigate to the i386 directory and install postfix and two other packages found inside the folder (postfix_debuginfo and pflogsumm)

> #cd /usr/src/redhat /RPMS/i386

> #rpm - ivh postfix - 2.2.8-1.2.i386.rpm

The installation required some dependencies depending on the installed packages your system, so you should download and install them then try reinstalling postfix.

### 3.2 Initial Configuration of Postfix:

To configure Postfix, the following lines are edited and uncommented in the /etc/postfix/main.cf file. Postfix is made aware of the fully qualified name and the local domain name of the server. Also given the server's outbound domain name that will be used when the emails sent by the server, what Ethernet interfaces will be allowed to accept, and the email clients IP addresses that are allowed to log in locally in the network .

> myhostname =project.uniswa.com

> mydomain =uniswa.com

> myorigin =$myhostname

> inet_interfaces = all

> mydestination = $myhostname, localhost.$mydomain, localhost

> mynetworks_style = subnet


To test if this was a success do the following:

> #service postfix restart

> #telnet localhost 25      // an output similar to the one below will come up

> Trying 127.0.0.1 …

> Connected to localhost.localdomain (127.0.0.1)

> Escape character is '^].

> 220 project.uniswa.com ESMTP Postfix

```
mail from: xyz
rcpt to: root@project.uniswa.sz
data
Hi testing
.
quit
```

## 3.3 Installing MySQL packages:

Install MySQL, mysql-devel, mysql-server, mysql-client packages from the RPMS that come with Fedora along with any dependency packages. To install for example mysql, write

```
# rpm –ivh mysql-*.rpm
```

## 3.4 Creating MySQL Tables:

Inside the MySQL shell, the Postfix and Postfix Admin users and passwords are created and given privileges to use Postfix. Here the table structure for MySQL that you need in order to configure Postfix Admin and Postfix in general to work with Virtual Domains and Users.

#mysql

Mysql> USE mysql;

To create Postfix user & password :

Mysql>INSERT INTO user (Host, User, Password) VALUES ('localhost', 'postfix'. password ('postfix');

INSERT INT db (Host, Db, User, Select_priv) VALUES ('localhost', 'postfix', 'Y');

To create Postfixadmin user & password:

Mysql> INSERT INTO user (Host, User, Password) VALUES ('localhost', 'postfixadmin', password ('postfixadmin'))

Mysql>INSERT INTO db (Host,Db,User,Select_priv,Insrte_priv,updata_priv,delete_priv) values ('local host','postfix','postfixadmin','Y','Y','Y','Y');

Mysql>FLUSH PRIVILEGES;

Mysql>GRANT USAGE ON postfix.* TO postfix@localhost;

Mysql>GRANT SELECT, INSERT, DELETE, UPDATE, CREATE, ALTER ON postfix.* TO postfix@localhost;

Mysql>GRANT USAGE ON postfix.* TO postfixadmin@localhost;

Mysql>GRANT SELECT, INSERT, DELETE, UPDATE, CREATE, ALTER ON postfix.* TO postfixadmin@localhost;

To create database postfix:

Still on the MySQL shell, create the database Postfix and the tables that Postfix and courier need.

Mysql> CREATE DATABASE postfix;

Mysql> USE postfix;

Now the needed database and useres have been added and given the correct permissions. Add the Postfix tables now.

The admin table will store information about the postfixadmin administrator. Table structure for table admin

Mysql> CREATE TABLE admin (username varchar (255) NOT NULL default".password varchar (255) NOT NULL default", Created datetime NOT NULL default '0000-00-00 00:00:00', Modified datetime default '0000-00-00 00:00:00', Active tinyint (1) NOT NULL default '1', PRIMARY KEY (username), KEY username (username)) TYPE = MYISAM COMMENT ='Postfix Admin – Virtual Admins',

The alias table is for aliasing one email address to another, e.g. forward emails for billfo@acme.com to johns@eeng.com. The table structure for table alias

Mysql>CREATE TABLE alias (address varchar (255) NOT NULL default", go to text NOT NULL, domain varchar (255) NOT NULL default", Created datetime NOT NULL default '0000-00-00 00:00:00', Modified datetime default '0000-00-00 00:00:00', active tinyint (1) NOT NULL default '1', PRIMARY KEY (username), KEY username (username)) TYPE = MYISAM COMMENT ='Postfix Admin – Virtual Aliases',

The domain table will store each virtual domain that Postfix should receive emails for (e.g. mtn.com). The table structure for table domain

Mysql> CREATE TABLE domain ( domain varchar (255) NOT NULL default", description varchar (255) NOT NULL default", Aliases int (10) NOT NULL default'0',

Mailboxes int (10) NOT NULL default '0', Maxquota int (10) NOT NULL default '0',

transport varchar (255) default NULL", backupmx tinyint (1) NOT NULL default '1',

11

Created datetime NOT NULL default '0000-00-00 00:00:00', Modified datetime default '0000-00-00 00:00:00', active tinyint (1) NOT NULL default '1', PRIMARY KEY (domain), KEY username (domain)) TYPE = MYISAM COMMENT ='Postfix Admin – Virtual Domains';

The domain_admins table will store information about domain administrators. The table structure for domain_admins

Mysql> CREATE TABLE domain_admins ( username varchar (255) NOT NULL default", domain varchar (255) NOT NULL default", Create datetime NOT NULL default '0000-00-00 00:00:00', Modified datetime default '0000-00-00 00:00:00', active tinyint (1) NOT NULL default '1', KEY username (username)) TYPE = MYISAM COMMENT ='Postfix Admin – Domains Admins',

The log table will store the time of activity for each virtual domain and user. The table structure for table log

Mysql> CREATE TABLE log (timestamp datetime NOT NULL default '0000-00-00 00:00:00', Username varchar (255) NOT NULL default", Domain varchar (255) NOT NULL default", Action varchar (255) NOT NULL default", Data varchar (255) NOT NULL default", KEY timestamp (timestamp)) TYPE = MYISAM COMMENT ='Postfix Admin – Log'

The mailbox table stores all virtual users (i.e. email addresses, because the email address and user name is the same), passwords (in encrypted form) and the quota value for each mailbox. The table structure for table mailbox

Mysql> CREATE TABLE mailbox ( username varchar(255) NOT NULL default ", password varchar(255) NOT NULL default ", name varchar(255) NOT NULL default ", maildir varchar(255) NOT NULL default ", quota int(10) NOT NULL default '0', domain varchar(255) NOT NULL default ", created datetime NOT NULL default '0000-00-00 00:00:00', modified datetime NOT NULL default '0000-00-00 00:00:00', active tinyint(1) NOT NULL default '1', PRIMARY KEY (username), KEY username (username) ) TYPE=MyISAM COMMENT='Postfix Admin - Virtual Mailboxes';

Virtual Vacation is done with a local shell account that can receive email. The email is then handled by a Perl script which sends the Vacation message back to the sender. The table structure for table vacation

Mysql> CREATE TABLE vacation (email varchar (255) NOT NULL default", subject varchar (255) NOT NULL default", body text   NOT NULL default", cache text   NOT NULL default", domain varchar (255) NOT NULL default", Created datetime NOT NULL default '0000-00-00 00:00:00', Active tinyint (1) NOT NULL default '1', PRIMARY KEY (email), KEY email (email), TYPE = MYISAM COMMENT ='Postfix Admin – virtual vacation';

The transport table is optional, it is for advanced users. It allows to forward mails for single users, whole domains or all mails to another server. The table structure for transport

Mysql> CREATE TABLE transport (username varchar (255) NOT NULL default", domain varchar (255) NOT NULL default", destination varchar (255) NOT NULL default", Created datetime NOT NULL default '0000-00-00 00:00:00', Modified datetime default '0000-00-00 00:00:00', active tinyint (1) NOT NULL default '1', PRIMARY KEY (domain));

## 3.5 Populating database with some data:

Next, the Postfix database has to be filled with some data which otherwise can still be filled through Postfixadmin.

#mysql

Mysql> Use postfix;

Mysql> INSERT INTO domain (domain, description) VALUES ('uniswa.com', 'Test Domain');
Mysql> INSERT INTO alias (address, goto) VALUES ('alias@uniswa.com', 'user@uniswa.com ');

Mysql> INSERT INTO mailbox (username, password, name, quota, maildir) VALUES ('user@uniswa.com', ENCRYPT(password),'Mailbox User','104857600', 'user@uniswa.com/');

quit;

## 3.6 Creating Postfix-MySql Configuration Files:

Postfix has to be told where to find all the information in the database. Therefore six access text files have to be created and mapped in etc/main.cf file to allow postfix to read from MySQL tables.

Create /etc/postfix/mysql/mysql_virtual_alias_maps.cf

user = postfix

password = postfix

host = localhost

dname = postfix

query =SELECT go to FROM alias WHERE address ='%s' AND active =1

Create /etc/postfix/mysql/mysql_virtual_domains_maps.cf

user = postfix

password = postfix

host = localhost

dname = postfix

query = SELECT domain FROM domain WHERE domain = '%s'

#optimal query to use when relaying for backup MX

Create /etc/postfix/mysql/mysql_virtual_mailbox_maps.cf

user = postfix

password = postfix

host = localhost

dname = postfix

query =SELECT maildir FROM mailbox WHERE username ='%s' AND active =1

Create /etc/postfix/mysql/mysql_virtual_mailbox_limit_maps.cf

user = postfix

password = postfix

host = localhost

dname = postfix

query =SELECT quota FROM mailbox WHERE username ='%s'

Create /etc/postfix/mysql/mysql_relay_domains_maps.cf

user = postfix

password = postfix

host = localhost

dname = postfix

query =SELECT domain FROM domain WHERE domain='%s' backupmx = '1'

Create /etc/postfix/mysql/transport_maps.cf

user = postfix

password = postfix

host = localhost

dname = postfix

table = transport

select_ field = destination

where_ field =domain

additional_conditions= and active = 'true'


### 3.7 Creating Virtual User and Virtual Directory:

The system can hold mailboxes for thousands of users. All of these users are virtual users and none of them is a Linux system user. One would probably do not want to assign a unique UID (user ID) to every user, so let's create a Linux user who will become the owner of all mailboxes.

The virtual postfix user with id = 89 and a folder named /vmail are created and made to own mail. The user is given permissions to read and write mail.

# mkdir /vmail

# chown –R postfix: postfix /vmail

#chmod –R 771 /vmail


### 3.8 Configuring Postfix with MySQL maps:

The six MySQL maps configuration files have already been created and now is the time to setup Postfix main.cf file so that Postfix can query MySQL database for virtual mailboxes and domains. Open the main.cf file.

# gedit /etc/postfix/main.cf

Then add the following code segment to main.cf

virtual_mailbox_ domains = mysql:/etc/postfix/mysql/mysql_virtual_domains_maps.cf

virtual_ alias_maps =mysql:/etc/postfix/mysql/mysql_virtual_alias_maps.cf

virtual_mailbox_maps =mysql:/etc/postfix/mysql/mysql_virtual_mailbox_maps.cf

Then the user id and group id of the user that will deliver mail to the virtual mailbox directory are assigned and the mailbox limit is declared.

virtual_gid_maps = static: 89

virtual_mailbox_limit =51200000

virtual _ uid_maps = static: 89

virtual_minimum_uid =10

virtual_ transport =virtual

These configurations are made for quota support

virtual_create_maildirsize =yes

virtual_mailbox_extended =yes

virtual_mailbox_limit_maps= mysql:/etc/postfix/mysql/mysql_virtual_mailbox_limit_maps.cf

virtual_mailbox_limit_ override= yes

virtual_maildir_limit_message =Sorry, the user's maildir has overdrawn his diskspace quota, please try again later.

virtual_overquota_bounce =yes


## 3.9 Installing Courier-IMAP and Courier-authlib:

The POP3 service enables a server to host e-mail accounts and includes tools to administer the servers, domains, and mailboxes. The POP3 service performs the tasks of message download and request handling on a server, where message download consists of transmitting the messages from a folder in the file system to clients and request handling is performed according to the POP3 protocol, which defines how the server responds to requests sent from an e-mail client.

The SMTP service receives e-mail from other domains, saves the e-mail to the Queue folder, and notifies the SMTP delivery service for POP3 of the arrival of e-mail. The delivery service then moves the e-mail to the POP3 mail store, where it is available for download to POP3 e-mail clients.

To install Courier –Imap, a regular system user other than the Root user has to be created because root dismally fails to build this package.

#useradd test   (creating a user called test)

#passwd test   (you can put any password)

#/bin/su -test    (changing to user test)

Create an RPM development hierarchy.

#mkdir $ HOME /rpm

#mkdir $ HOME/rpm/SOURCES

#mkdir $ HOME/rpm/ SPECS

#mkdir $ HOME/rpm/ BUILD

#mkdir $ HOME/rpm/SRPMS

#mkdir $ HOME/rpm/RPMS

#mkdir $ HOME/rpm/RPMS/i386

#echo "%_topdir $HOME/rpm">>$HOME/.rpmmacros

Download courier-imap tarball (old version that can be used with Fedora 5), and save it in /home/test/rpm/SOURCES directory and unpack it

#cp courier-imap-4.4.1.tar.bz2 /home/test/rpm/SOURCES

#cd /home/rpm/SOURCES

#tar xjf courier-imap-4.4.1.tar.bz2

Go to /home/test/rpm/sources/courier-imap-4.4.1 and edit the specification file

# cd courier-imap-4.0.1

# gedit courier-imap.spec

Change the following lines to have things in more standard places ( eg. /etc )
%define _sysconfdir /etc/courier
%define _mandir /usr/share/man
%define _prefix /etc/courier
%define _localstatedir /var/run
%configure \
--with-redhat \
--enable-workaround-for-imap-client-bugs \
%{?xflags: %{xflags}}
       #%{__make} check

After editing, copy the courier-imap.spec file to /home/test/rpm/SPECS directory. Before building the courier-imap, it is required that courier–authlib package (for authentication) is installed. Download

17

courier-authlib-0.62.1.tar.bz2 or any suitable version and save it in the SOURCES directory. Unpack it and edit the specification file, then copy it to /home/test/rpm/SPECS directory, build it and install it as root in the i386 directory.

#cp courier-authlib-0.62.1.tar.bz2 /home/test/rpm/SOURCES

#cd /home/rpm/SOURCES

#tar xjf courier-authlib-0.59.1.tar.bz2

Install the courier-authlib

#cd $HOME/rpm/SPECS

#rmpbuild - bb courier - authlib. spec

#su root

#cd/home/test/rpm/RPMS/i356/

# rpm-ivh courier-authlib-*

It asks for libtool-itdl-devel as a failed dependency, install it and install any other required dependencies after downloading them. You shall install all courier-authlib packages found in the i386 folder if you want your courier-imap to support them. You will find there the following packages:courier_authlib, courier_authlib_devel, courier_authlib_debuginfo, courier_authlib_userdb, courier_authlib_mysql, courier_authlib_pgsql, courier_authlib_userdb_ldab.


Build the courier–imap package as user test and install it as root user.

#su test

#cd $HOME/rpm/SPECS

#rpmbuilb-bb courier-imap.spec

#su root

#cd/home/test/rpm/RPMS/i386/

#rpm-ivh courier-imap-*

Install any failed dependencies as required. Then start the package as follows:

#authdaemond restart

#service courier-authlib restart

18

#service courier-imap restart

### 3.10  Courier-IMAP Configuration:

To tell Courier that it should authenticate against the MySQL database, first edit /etc/authlib/authdaemonrc and change the value of authmodulelist so that it reads from mysql database.

Authmodulelist = "authmysql"

The Courier- Imap imapd file /etc/courier/imapd should have a line similar to this,
IMAP_CAPABILITY ="IMAP4rev 1 UIDPLUS CHILDREN NAMESPACE

THREAD = ORDEREDSUBJECT THREAD= REFERENCES SORT QUOTA IDLE"

The 'authmysqlrc' file in /etc/authlib directory is edited and modified and these lines added to it:

#DEFAULT _DOMAIN    uniswa.com

MYSQL_CRYPT_PWFIELD  password

MYSQL_ DATABASE    postfix

MYSQL_GID_FIELD    '89'

MYSQL_HOME_FIELD   '/vmail/'

MYSQL_ LOGIN _FIELD   username

MYSQL_MAILDIR_FIELD    maildir

MYSQL_NAME _FIELD     name

MYSQL_OPT     0

MYSQL_ PASSWORD    postfix

#MYSQL_ PORT    0

#Uncomment below for quota support.

MYQL_QUOTA_FIELD quota

MYSQL_ SERVER    localhost

#Default RedHat Socket

MYSQL _SOCKET   /var/lib/mysql. Sock

MYSQL_UID_FIELD   '89'

MYSQL_USERNAME   postfix

MYSQL_USER _TABLE   mailbox

#MYSQL _WHER_CLAUSE   server = 'project.uniswa.com'


A file /etc/authlib/hostdomains is created that contains **uniswa.com**, the domain that will be hosted by this server.

For testing with courier-imap
        # service postfix reload
        # authdaemond restart
        # service courier-authlib restart
        # service courier-imap restart
        # telnet localhost 25
        mail from: hedaya
        rcpt to: user@uniswa.com
        data
        hi testing
        .
        quit

        # telnet localhost 110
        user user@uniswa.com
        pass password
        list
        retr (msg no)
        quit

### 3.11 Configuring Postfixadmin:

Postfix will allow the administrator to add, delete and edit mailboxes and full domains. This web based application allows the administrator to access MySQL configuration for postfix and edits it directly .The prerequisite for the installation of Postfixadmin is to install Apache. Postfix tar is downloaded from http://high5.net and saved in the apache directory /var/www/html and then unarchive it.

> #tar –zxvf postfixadmin-*.tar.gz

The following configurations are performed in the config.inc.php file.

The first thing to do is to tell Postfix that you have configured the application.

```
$CONF['configured'] = true;
```

Then the full url of the postfix admin build is defined.

```
$CONF ['postfix_admin_url'] = 'http: //uniswa.com/postfixadmin';
```

Next is the setting up of the database connection.

```
$CONF ['database_type'] = 'mysql';
$CONF ['database_host'] = 'localhost';
$CONF ['database_user'] = 'postfixadmin';
$CONF ['database_password'] = 'postfixadmin';
$CONF ['database_name'] = 'postfix';
$CONF ['database_prefix'] = ;
```

The email address that all problems will be reported to and the sends messages to everyone.

```
$CONF ['admin_email'] = 'postmaster@example.com';
```

This is used to send email to Postfix in order to create mailboxes.

```
$CONF ['smtp_server'] = 'localhost';
$CONF ['smtp_port'] = '25';
```

This portion defines the encryption method to be used to encrypt passwords.

```
$CONF ['encrypt'] = 'md5';
```

This will be assigned during the postfixadmin Superadmin setup.

```
$CONF ['setup_password'] = '';
```

Minimum length required for passwords.

```
$CONF ['min_password_length'] = 5;
```

21

The default aliases that need to be created for all domains.

```
$CONF ['default_aliases'] = array (
    'postmaster' => 'postmaster@example.com',
);
```

This part is set to 'yes' if the mailboxes are to be stored per domain, otherwise it is set to 'no'.

```
$CONF ['domain_path'] = 'YES';
```

This is set to 'no' if putting the domain in the mailbox is not desired.

```
$CONF ['domain_in_mailbox'] = 'YES';
```

This specifies the quota value in MB.

```
$CONF ['aliases'] = '10';
$CONF ['mailboxes'] = '10';
$CONF ['maxquota'] = '10';
```

To enforce quota for mailbox users this is set to 'yes'.

```
$CONF['quota'] = 'YES';
```

There are two choices, either use '1024000' or '1048576'

```
$CONF ['quota_multiplier'] = '1024000';
```

If there is a need to define additional transport options for a domain this is set to 'yes'.

```
$CONF ['transport'] = 'YES';
```

If additional transport options are to be defined, they should be put in the array below.

```
$CONF ['transport_options'] = array (
    'virtual',  // for virtual accounts
    'local',    // for system accounts
    'relay'     // for backup mx
);
```

Transport default

```
$CONF ['transport_default'] = 'virtual';
```

PostfixAdmin inserts an alias in the alias table for every mailbox it creates. The reason for this is that when you want catch-all and normal mailboxes to work you need to have the mailbox replicated in the alias table. If you want to take control of these aliases as well set this to 'yes'.

$CONF ['alias control'] = 'YES';

Alias Control for admins.

$CONF ['alias_control_admin'] = 'YES';

This message is sent to every newly created mailbox.

$CONF ['welcome_text'] = <<<EOM
Hi,

Welcome to your new account.
EOM;

Next go to the URL that you have set in PostfixAdmin, and go to the setup page.

In Mozilla Firefox browser type the URL http://uniswa.com/postfixadmin/setup.php, travel down to the bottom of the page and create a strong 'setup password' by only using the password form and hit enter. Copy the hashed output presented and paste it into the postfixadmin configuration file on the appropriate line that has $conf [setup_password]

Create a super admin account with an email address and admin password, by using the setup password that has just been used to generate the hash output. If everything is correct, the setup will create the admin database. Now super admin will be able to access Postfixadmin management through http://uniswa.com/postfixadmin/admin/. The figures below show the postfixadmin interface. Fig. 3.1 shows the screen presented in postfixadmin/setup.php to set up the Superadmin account. Fig. 3.2 shows the screen presented to log into administration site of postfixadmin in postfixadmin/admin/. Fig. 3.3 shows the screen after logging into the admin site and choosing Domain List.

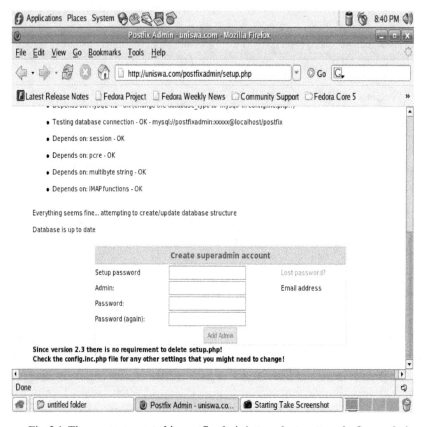

Fig. 3.1. The screen presented in postfixadmin/setup.php to set up the Superadmin account.

**Fig. 3.2. The screen presented to log into dministration site of postfixadmin in postfixadmin/admin/.**

25

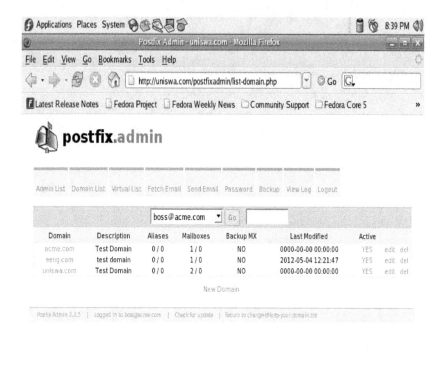

**Figure 3.3**

**The screen after logging into the admin site and choosing domain list.**

### 3.12  Configuring Squirrelmail:

This is a client web mail interface that users use to access their mail.

1-Download squirrelmail from www.squirrelmail.org. Download for example squirrelmail-1.4.6.tar.bz2 or any other version.

2-Extract the squirrelmail

3-Copy the squirrelmail to folder /var/www/html/squirrelmail

6-Change to directory /var/www/squirrelmail/config

7-Rename the file config_default.php to config.php

8-Create directories /var/www/html/squirrelmail/attach and /var/www/html/squirrelmail/data, and change their ownership

> # chown –R apache data

> # chgrp- R apache data

> # chown – R apache attach

> #chgrp –R apache attach

> # chmod 730 data

> #chmod 730 attach

9- Download a quota usage plugin from squirrel site to /var/www/html/squirrelmail/plugins.

> # cd /var/www/hml/squirrelmail/plugins

> # tar –zxvf quota_usage-1.3-1.2.7.tar.gz

10- Change into the quota_ usage directory, copy config.php.sample to config.php and edit config.php, making adjustments as you deem necessary.

> # cd quota_usage

> #cp config.php.sample config.php

9- From the command line at /var/www/html/squirrelmail/config, excute perl script

> #./config.pl

> Choose 2. Server Setting Change Domain:

Choose 4. General Option, Change attachment directory to.../attach/, Change data directory to .../data/

Choose 8. Plug- in, Add all plug-in including quota _usage

Choose S to save the configuration

10- Restart httpd service

    # Service httpd restart

11- In browser, browse http://project.uniswa.com/squirrelmail/

### 3.13  Installing and Configuring MailScanner, ClamAV and SpamAssassin :

Postfix puts all incoming email into a hold queue so Mailscanner can safely access these emails for scanning and then pass them back to the Postfix active queue for delivery. I downloaded Mailscanner from http://www.mailscanner.info/downloads.html. After unpacking the package, it will create a new directory. Move into the new directory using the "cd" command, then run the command
    # ./install.sh

This will produce a very large amount of output, as it tries to build and install all the packages that MailScanner uses. If not, you should first install all dependency packages that MailScanner uses.

Here are the options you will need to change in the MailScanner configuration file.
    %org-name% = yoursite
    Run As User = postfix
    Run As Group = postfix
    Incoming Queue Dir = /var/spool/postfix/hold
    Outgoing Queue Dir = /var/spool/postfix/incoming
    MTA = postfix
    Virus Scanning = yes
    Virus Scanners = clamav
    Spam List = spamhaus.org spamcop.net ORDB-RBL
    Use SpamAssassin = yes

The best way for proper installation of ClamAV and SpamAssassin is through the package that was prepared specially for this purpose in www.mailscanner.info. Download the package from http://www.mailscanner.info/files/4/install-Clam-0.88.7-SA-3.1.7.tar.gz or any other version.

You need to unpack the tar file, move into the new directory using the "cd" command, then run the command
    # ./install.sh

You can adjust the file freshclam.conf to suite your proxy setting,

28

UpdateLogFile /var/log/freshclam.log
HTTPProxyServer proxy.uniswa.sz
HTTPProxyPort 80

To start clamav and spanassassin, run
# service spamd start
# clamd start

For auto update, run
# freshclam


We will need to edit postfix to hold all email messages so that MailScanner can scan them and then put them in the mail queue. The following line should be added to /etc/postfix/main.cf
header_checks = regexp:/etc/postfix/header_checks

Then we will need to create the header_checks file /etc/postfix/header_checks and put in this information:
/^Received:/ HOLD

You will need to ensure that the user "postfix" can write to /var/spool/MailScanner/incoming and /var/spool/MailScanner/quarantine:
# chown postfix.postfix /var/spool/MailScanner/incoming
# chown postfix.postfix /var/spool/MailScanner/quarantine


To start MailScanner, run
# service MailScanner start


The problem is that the MailScanner could not be loaded successfully after starting and so that part of project could be implemented successfully. The emails could not be scanned for spams and viruses.

# 4 Testing the configuration:

For testing the configurations go, to root directory and do the following steps:

#service postfix reload

#authdaemond restart

#service courier-authlib restart

#service courier-imap restart

# service mysqld restart

# service httpd restart

# telnet localhost 25
mail from: khumalo
rcpt to: user@uniswa.com
data
just testing
.
quit

# telnet localhost 110
user user@uiswa.com
pass password
list
retr (msg no)
quit

Testing is done in the Linux shell first using commands as shown in Fig. 4.1 and Fig. 4.2 below.

Then open Mozilla Firefox and connect to http://project.uniswa.com/squirrelmail/ to test the mail server using the graphical interface squirrelmail as shown in Fig. 4.3, Fig. 4.4, Fig. 4.5, Fig. 4.6 and Fig. 4.7. Fig. 4.3 shows user bob@uniswa.com logs into the system. Fig. 4.4 shows user bob@uniswa.com composes mail to user bill@acme.com. Fig. 4.5 shows user bill@acme.com logs to the system. Fig. 6 shows user bill@acme.com is notified of his new mail from user bob@uniswa.com. Fig. 4.7. shows user bill@acme.com reads his mail from user bob@uniswa.com

As the installation of MailScanner was not successful, testing the mail server in scanning viruses and spams was not possible.

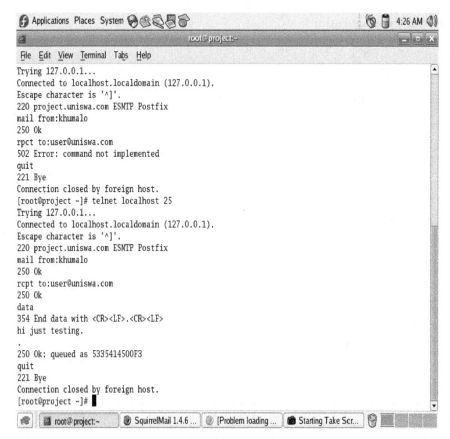

Fig. 4.1. Testing the email server using command lines, user khumalo is sending mail to user@uniswa.com.

**Fig. 4.2. Testing the email server using command lines, user@uniswa.com reads his mail from khumalo**

**Figure 4.3. Testing logging to mail server through squirrelmail, user bob@uniswa.com logs into the system**

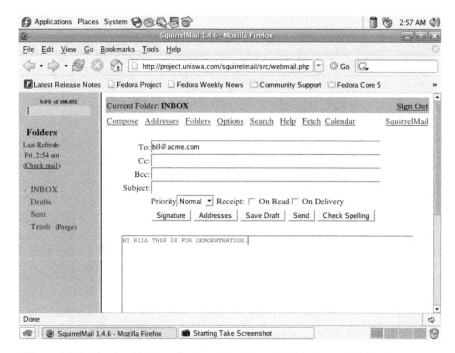

**Figure 4.4. Testing logging to mail server through squirrelmail, user bob@uniswa.com composes mail to user bill@acme.com**

**Figure 4.5. Testing logging to mail server through squirrelmail, user bill@acme.com logs to the system**

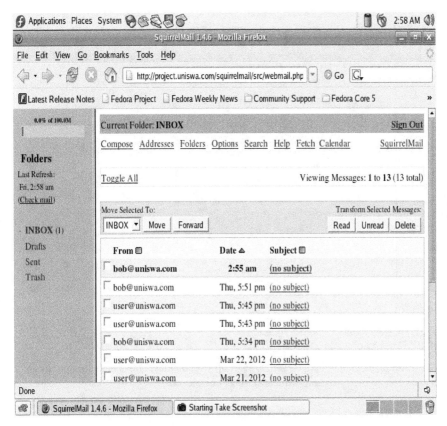

Figure 4.6. Testing logging to mail server through squirrelmail, user bill@acme.com is notified of his new mail from user bob@uniswa.com

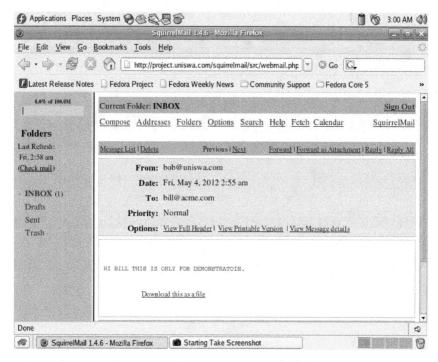

Figure 4.7. Testing logging to mail server through squirrelmail, user bill@acme.com reads his mail from user bob@uniswa.com

## 5 Conclusion:

The initial objective of this work was to build an email server that supports mail delivery to multiple virtual domains where each email address will be authentic to its own domain. It has been demonstrated that by following the configuration steps that involve building and installing rpm packages in the Linux command line this can be achieved.

Further more the administration of the domains and users proved to be easy when using the Postfixadmin web tool as compared to doing it inside the MySQL shell using SQL commands. Using the squirrelmail webmail interface made it simple for users to send and retrieve mail instead of doing it in the command line where one is supposed to always remember all the necessary commands.

The security part of the system proved to be the down side in the whole system. There has not been sufficient time to fully integrate the scanning of the mail and killing of the spam and viruses. Although the installation of the anti virus and anti spam was successful integrating these with the mail scanner was more of a challenge, work is ongoing and there is hope that meaningful progress will be realized to allow for the demonstration of this part of the work.

The experience gained during the implementation of the system has provided immense knowledge in the behavior and working of Linux servers in general and also with the MySQL server.

www.ingramcontent.com/pod-product-compliance
Lightning Source LLC
LaVergne TN
LVHW052125070326
832902LV00038B/3951

ISBN 9781984047885

90000 >

9 781984 047885